America Goes to War

The Spanish-American War

by Kerry A. Graves

Consultant:
Stephen E. Osman
Historic Fort Snelling, Minnesota

CAPSTONE BOOKS

an imprint of Capstone Pres~
Mankato, Minnesota

AUG 2 4 2001

Capstone Books are published by Capstone Press,
151 Good Counsel Drive, P.O. Box 669, Mankato, Minnesota 56002.
www.capstonepress.com

Library of Congress Cataloging-in-Publication Data
Graves, Kerry A.
    The Spanish-American War/by Kerry A. Graves.
    p. cm.—(America goes to war)
    Includes bibliographical references and index.
    Summary: Examines the events leading up to the Spanish-American War, the life
of the soldiers, major battles, and the outcome of the war.
    ISBN 0-7368-0583-4 (hardcover)
    ISBN 0-7368-8859-4 (paperback)
    1. Spanish-American War, 1898—Juvenile literature. [1. Spanish-American War,
1898.] I. Title. II. Series
E715.G73 2001
973.8'9—dc21   00-025823

Editorial Credits
Blake Hoena, editor; Timothy Halldin, cover designer and illustrator; Katy Kudela,
    photo researcher

Photo Credits
Archive Photos, cover, 11, 15, 17, 19, 20, 23, 25, 26, 29, 36, 40
North Wind Photo Archives, 6, 8, 12, 30, 34
U.S. Army Military History Institute, 39

2 3 4 5 6 06 05 04 03 02

Table of Contents

Features

Fast Facts

Name and Dates: The Spanish-American War officially began April 25, 1898, and ended December 10, 1898.

Issue of the War: Cuban revolutionary groups wanted their independence from Spain. The United States supported these rebels. Cuba and Spain could not settle their differences peacefully.

Start of the War: On February 15, 1898, the battleship *Maine* exploded in Havana, Cuba's harbor. American newspapers blamed Spain for this disaster. Public pressure then forced President McKinley to declare war against Spain.

Battle Locations: Most battles took place on the island of Cuba. This island is located 90 miles (145 kilometers) south of Florida. Other battles occurred in the Philippines, Guam, and Puerto Rico. These islands were all Spanish territories at the beginning of the war.

Major Battles: Battle of Manila Bay (May 1898); Battle of Guantánamo (June 1898); Battle of Las Guásimas (June 1898); Battles of El Caney and San Juan Hill (July 1898); Battle of Santiago (July 1898)

Important Leaders:

United States: President William McKinley; Admiral George Dewey; Commodore William Sampson; Commodore Winfield Schley; Major General Nelson Miles; Major General William Shafter; Major General Joseph Wheeler; Colonel Theodore Roosevelt

Spain: Queen Regent María Cristina; Governor of Cuba, General Blanco; Governor-General in the Philippine Islands, Basilo Augustín Dávila; Admiral Patricio Montojo y Pasaron; Admiral Pascual Cervera y Topete; General Firmín Jaudenes; General José Toral

Cuba: Lieutenant General Calixto García Iñiguez

Philippines: General Emilio Aguinaldo

Weapons Used: Battleships; rifles; Gatling guns; artillery; mines; barbed wire

End of the War: Spanish and U.S. officials signed the Treaty of Peace in Paris, France, on December 10, 1898.

Chapter 1

Before the War

In the 1800s, Cuba was a colony of Spain. Spanish leaders made laws for Cubans. Spanish soldiers in Cuba enforced these laws. Cubans had little control over their own lives and freedom.

Ten Years' War

In 1868, Cubans rebelled against Spanish rule. Their fight for independence was called the Ten Years' War (1868–1878).

Many U.S. citizens heard about this war and supported the Cuban rebels. Some Americans even sent money and weapons to the rebels.

Neither side won the Ten Years' War. In 1878, Spanish leaders ended the fighting by promising to improve living conditions for Cubans.

Cuban rebels fought for independence from Spanish rule.

In 1895, a new revolution began in Cuba.

But the Spanish leaders did not keep their promises. Instead, they arrested, killed, and exiled Cubans for their ideas. Exiled Cubans were forced to leave their homes.

Some Cubans moved to the United States to escape the harsh living conditions in Cuba. Many of them joined exiled Cubans already in the United States. Together, these people formed the Cuban Revolutionary Party. This group raised money for weapons and planned another revolution to free Cuba from Spanish rule.

Rebellion in 1895

In 1895, the Cuban Revolutionary Party began a new revolution. Many Cuban rebels returned to Cuba to fight in this war.

Spanish leaders decided to prevent Cuban villagers from helping the rebels. Villagers often supplied rebels with food. They also cared for wounded rebels. Spanish leaders began the "reconcentrado" camp system. They gathered villagers into central camps and burned their farms and villages.

Camp conditions were poor. Many Cubans became sick or starved in these camps. One out of every eight Cubans died in the camps during the revolution. These terrible conditions attracted the attention of people in the United States.

Issues of the War

The U.S. government was concerned about the war in Cuba. The island is only 90 miles (145 kilometers) south of Florida. U.S. businessmen had invested millions of dollars in Cuba's sugar industry. Many U.S. citizens also lived and worked in Cuba.

In January 1898, riots in Havana, Cuba, destroyed shops and endangered U.S. citizens living there. Rumors also spread that Spanish soldiers planned to murder U.S. citizens.

The Battleship *Maine*

At the time, William McKinley was president of the United States. He did not want to start a war with Spain. But McKinley wanted to prevent U.S. citizens from being harmed in Cuba.

Spanish leaders hoped to prevent war. But they also did not want to lose Cuba as a colony. Spanish leaders decided to release Cubans from the camps. They also offered Cuban leaders power to make some national decisions. But Cuban leaders wanted complete control of their government. They refused this offer.

McKinley ordered the battleship *Maine* to sail to Havana's harbor. McKinley hoped its presence would prevent U.S. citizens from being harmed.

On February 15, 1898, an explosion erupted in Havana's harbor. This explosion sunk the *Maine* and killed 266 sailors aboard the ship. U.S. Navy investigators could not discover what caused the explosion.

The battleship *Maine* was destroyed in Havana's harbor.

Many people in the United States blamed the explosion on Spain. U.S. newspapers ran stories accusing Spain of sinking the *Maine*. These stories were untrue. But many U.S. citizens believed them and wanted the United States to go to war with Spain. Many U.S. politicians also spoke against Spain. They supported Cubans in their revolution. In April 1898, McKinley asked Congress to declare war on Spain.

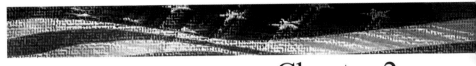

Chapter 2

A Call to Arms

President McKinley knew that the U.S. Army would need more troops to fight a war. At the time, the army had less than 30,000 soldiers. In April 1898, McKinley asked for 125,000 volunteers to join the army.

Types of Soldiers

Most volunteers enlisted in one of three military units. These units were infantry, cavalry, and artillery units.

Most soldiers belonged to infantry units. These foot soldiers marched to battles carrying their weapons, ammunition, and personal items.

Cavalry troops rode horses. They could move more quickly than infantry soldiers. Cavalry troops often scouted for enemy forces.

President McKinley asked for volunteers to join the U.S. Army.

Artillery troops operated the cannons used in battles. Mule or horse teams pulled cannons and heavy-ammunition wagons to battle sites.

Other volunteers joined the navy. Sailors served on blockade, transport, and hospital ships during the war.

Strengths and Weaknesses

The U.S. Army had many problems to solve before it was ready to fight a war with Spain. The army included mostly inexperienced soldiers. Many military officers did not have any combat experience. The U.S. Army also had never landed large numbers of soldiers from ships onto a defended coast before.

Army officials had little information about their enemy. They did not know how many Spanish soldiers were in Cuba. They did not know where these soldiers were stationed. This lack of information made it difficult to plan an invasion.

The Spanish Army had some advantages. Its soldiers had been in Cuba for many years. They were familiar with the countryside. They had built stone and wooden forts for protection. Spanish soldiers also had more advanced

The U.S. Navy had more advanced warships than the Spanish Navy.

weapons than U.S. soldiers. Spanish soldiers had German Mauser rifles and Krupp cannons. These weapons used smokeless gunpowder. This allowed Spanish soldiers to fire their weapons from hidden positions and remain undetected.

The United States had an advantage at sea. New U.S. battleships were more advanced than Spanish ships. But the U.S. Navy did not have transport ships to take men and supplies to Cuba. It bought or rented ships from private owners and trade companies to transport troops.

Outfitting the Soldiers

U.S. soldiers received their uniforms and gear when they enlisted. But the military often did not have enough equipment for all new volunteers.

Army rules called for a color-coded cord on soldiers' hats. Infantry wore white cords. Artillery wore red cords. Cavalry wore yellow cords.

Soldiers also wore metal pins to identify their unit. Infantry pins had two crossed rifles. Cavalry pins had two crossed swords. Artillery pins showed two crossed cannons.

Soldiers also received other equipment. Canteens held soldiers' water supply. Soldiers carried a mess kit containing eating utensils. Soldiers also carried half of a two-man tent, a blanket, and extra clothes.

Soldiers used a variety of weapons. Five-shot Krag-Jörgensen rifles used smokeless gunpowder. But the army did not have enough of these rifles. Most new infantry volunteers received single-shot Springfield rifles. These rifles released a cloud of white smoke when fired. This allowed enemy troops to spot soldiers firing these rifles.

Artillery and cavalry troops carried other weapons. Cavalry soldiers used Krag carbines. These lightweight rifles had short barrels to

Cavalry soldiers rode horses.

make them easier to carry on horseback. Artillery
soldiers carried revolvers and curved swords
called sabers.

Battle Plans

In May 1898, President McKinley named Major
General Nelson Miles commander of the army.
Miles had a two-part plan for the attack on Cuba.
First, he wanted to train troops all summer. This
would give them more experience using their

weapons. He also wanted to avoid illnesses among the troops. Yellow fever was common in Cuba during the summer. In the fall, Miles then planned to send 50,000 troops to meet with Cuban rebels. These combined forces would attack the Spanish at Havana.

The second part of Miles' plan involved the navy. During the summer, U.S. ships would form a blockade around Cuban ports. The blockade would stop Spain from sending supplies to its soldiers in Cuba.

Blockade

Spanish leaders knew a blockade around Cuba meant disaster for their troops. Spanish soldiers would run out of supplies and ammunition. Spanish leaders then sent ships under Admiral Pascual Cervera y Topete's command to break the U.S. blockade around Cuba.

Two U.S. Navy squadrons were sent to search for Cervera's ships. Admiral William Sampson led one group of ships and sailed to San Juan, Puerto Rico. Commodore Winfield Schley led the second group of ships and searched in Cuban waters.

On May 27, Schley found Cervera's fleet in Santiago Bay. But Schley was unable to attack

Admiral Cervera commanded the Spanish fleet.

these ships. Spanish artillery protected the bay's entrance. Two days later, Sampson arrived and added his ships to the blockade of the bay.

Spanish actions forced U.S. military leaders to change their plans. They decided to destroy Cervera's ships instead of attacking Havana in the fall. Cervera's ships could attack U.S. transport and supply ships traveling between Cuba and the United States. But the U.S. Navy was unable to fight the ships in the bay. That meant the U.S. Army would then have to attack Santiago. Artillery protecting the bay was stationed around this city.

Chapter 3

Early Battles

The first battle of the Spanish-American War did not occur in Cuba. U.S. ships attacked Spanish ships stationed in the Philippines. These Pacific islands were a Spanish colony.

On April 30, U.S. Commodore George Dewey led seven U.S. ships to Manila. This city is the capital of the Philippines. Dewey had orders to attack and prevent the Spanish fleet from sailing to Cuba. Admiral Patricio Montojo y Pasaron commanded the Spanish fleet.

On May 1, Dewey found Montojo's fleet located near the city of Cavite. The Spanish ships were older than the U.S. ships. Their cannons were not as powerful as the U.S. cannons. Dewey's fleet sunk all of the Spanish ships.

Commodore Dewey commanded U.S. ships in the Philippines.

5th Army Corps

On June 7, Major General William Shafter received orders to prepare soldiers of the 5th Army Corps. U.S. military officials had decided to attack Santiago, Cuba.

The 5th Army Corps consisted of nearly 17,000 soldiers. It was divided into two infantry divisions and one cavalry division. Each of these divisions were divided into smaller units called regiments. The 1st U.S. Volunteer Cavalry Regiment was well known before it had even reached Cuba. Many of the volunteers in this unit were ranchers, cowboys, and American Indians. People called this regiment the "Rough Riders." Theodore Roosevelt was a member of this unit.

Cuban Landing

The port of Tampa, Florida, became a busy place after troops were ordered to Cuba. U.S. transport ships were overcrowded with troops. Many supplies had to be left behind. These supplies included most of the horses for cavalry regiments. It took a week for the soldiers and supplies to be loaded onto transport ships.

On June 10, the first U.S. troops landed at Guantánamo. This village is in southeastern

U.S. transport ships were overcrowded with troops.

Cuba. U.S. soldiers attacked and defeated Spanish soldiers defending this village.

On June 20, Cuban rebel Lieutenant General Calixto García met with Shafter and Sampson. He told them safe places to land more troops. On June 22, Brigadier General Henry Lawton landed 6,000 men at the village of Daiquirí. This village is 17 miles (27 kilometers) east of Santiago.

The next day, Lawton led these soldiers toward the village of Siboney. The Rough

Riders were among these troops. U.S. soldiers built a camp at Siboney. Shafter had decided to make Siboney his headquarters. A road led from Siboney to Santiago. This would be the attack route that the 5th Army Corps would follow.

General Wheeler

Major General Joseph Wheeler commanded the cavalry division at Siboney. On June 23, he learned that Spanish soldiers blocked the road to Santiago. These troops were about 3 miles (4.8 kilometers) away at the village of Las Guásimas.

Wheeler did not have orders from Lawton. But he decided to lead an attack against the Spanish soldiers. On June 24, Wheeler and 1,000 cavalry soldiers advanced on foot.

The troops were inexperienced and unprepared for battle. The Spanish soldiers hid in the jungles surrounding the U.S. troops and attacked with smokeless rifles. U.S. troops were unable to see the Spanish soldiers and fire back.

After two hours, a U.S. infantry regiment arrived from Siboney. The Spanish soldiers then retreated and U.S. troops took control of Las Guásimas. After this victory, U.S. forces were only 6 miles (10 kilometers) from Santiago.

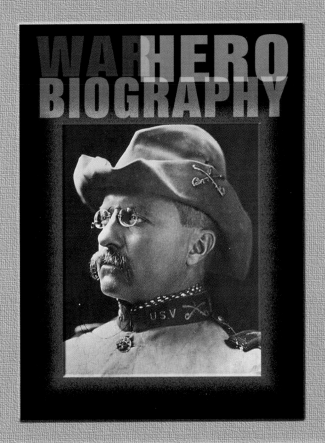

Theodore (Teddy) Roosevelt (1858–1919)

Roosevelt was born October 27, 1858, in New York City. He grew up listening to stories about the Civil War (1861–1865) and admired its heroes. In 1880, he graduated from Harvard. He was elected to the New York legislature (1882–1884) and served as a U.S. Civil Service commissioner (1889–1895). He also served as the president of the New York police board in 1895. In 1897, President Mckinley appointed Roosevelt the assistant navy secretary. But he resigned this post when the Spanish-American war began. Roosevelt then helped form the "Rough Riders." In 1900, he served as McKinley's vice president. After McKinley's assassination, Roosevelt become president (1901–1909). He died January 5, 1919.

Chapter 4

Life in Camp

Many volunteers never made it to battle. Only two of the seven army corps were sent to fight. U.S. Army leaders sent the 5th Army Corps to Cuba. They sent the 8th Army Corps to the Philippines. The rest of the soldiers reported to training camps and stayed there during the war.

Volunteer Camps

Many problems existed in the volunteer camps. Officers in volunteer camps often were not strict in enforcing rules to keep camps clean. Soldiers set tents too close together. They also did not maintain water-drainage trenches. This caused garbage dumps and outdoor toilets to flood when it rained. Water supplies then became contaminated. The dirty conditions led to

Many U.S. soldiers did not leave training camps during the Spanish-American War.

thousands of cases of typhoid fever, dysentery, and other diseases.

The Supply System

The shipment of supplies caused problems for the military. Inexperienced supply staff made many mistakes organizing both men and supplies.

Boxcars full of supplies crowded railroad lines. But supply officers did not have lists to tell them what was in each boxcar. They had to open each boxcar to find out what was inside. This took so long that much of the food supplies spoiled before they could be used.

The 5th Army Corps did not have enough ships. Thousands of troops had to be left behind. The 5th Army Corps also had to leave 60 cannons behind.

Leaving for Cuba

On June 14, 32 transport ships sailed for Cuba. They contained 819 officers and more than 15,000 soldiers.

Conditions aboard the ships were overcrowded. Two men were assigned to each bunk. Bunk beds had to be stacked three high. The heat aboard the ships made soldiers too uncomfortable to sleep.

Troops and supplies often were shipped by train.

Soldiers also did not have water to bathe during the trip. Solders stayed on these ships for more than a week.

Difficulties of War
In Cuba, soldiers did not receive their supplies regularly. Food often was spoiled when it arrived.

Soldiers began to realize the difficulties of war. At night, the ground was too damp to sleep on. Soldiers often had to bury fellow soldiers killed during battle.

The wounded often were treated at field hospitals.

Medical Care for the Wounded

After each battle, wounded soldiers had to be moved to a field hospital behind the battle lines. Field hospitals were large canvas tents. These tents included surgery and recovery tents. But the tents did not protect wounded soldiers from heat, dust, or insects during operations. Usually, only five surgeons worked at a hospital. They often worked many hours with few supplies.

Conditions at hospitals were poor. Many wounded soldiers lined up outside the tents.

They sometimes had to wait hours in the sun before being treated. Recovery tents often overflowed with wounded men. Patients then had to lay on the ground after their operations.

Nurses in the War

In 1898, only 720 nurses worked in the army. These nurses were all male. Before the Spanish-American War, the U.S. Army only hired male nurses.

The U.S. Army needed to hire more nurses when the war began. But there were not enough men to fill these positions. Most men had joined fighting units. More than a thousand women applied for the nursing jobs. In 1898, the Army Nurse Corps Division was formed. In 1901, the army formed a permanent women's Army Nurse Corps.

Spanish-American War nurses worked at various locations. Many worked in hospitals at training camps. Some were stationed in field hospitals in Puerto Rico, the Philippines, Cuba, and Hawaii. Others worked aboard hospital ships. Wounded soldiers were transported to these ships after they received treatment at a field hospital.

El Caney
Santiago Las Guásimas
Siboney
San Juan Hill Daiquirí
Guantánamo Bay

Tampa

N

W E

S

Gulf of Mexico

Havana

Cuba

Guantánamo
Santiago
Daiquirí

Caribbean Sea

Chapter 5

Final Battles

El Caney stood between Las Guásimas and Santiago. Spanish soldiers defended this stone fort. They also fortified San Juan Hill and Kettle Hill near El Caney. U.S. troops needed to attack the Spanish soldiers at these locations before advancing toward Santiago.

On June 30, Major General Shafter prepared his troops for battle. He ordered 5,000 soldiers to attack the Spanish troops at El Caney. At the same time, 8,000 U.S. soldiers would attack at San Juan Hill and Kettle Hill.

The fighting was difficult for U.S. troops. They had to climb narrow, muddy trails as Spanish soldiers fired down on them. Because of this, the battle at El Caney lasted nearly 10 hours. The Spanish troops then began to run out

U.S. troops had a difficult climb up San Juan Hill.

of ammunition and decided to retreat. The length of this battle kept U.S. troops at El Caney from helping attack San Juan Hill and Kettle Hill.

The Rough Riders helped attack the Spanish forces at Kettle Hill. U.S. troops forced these Spanish soldiers to retreat to San Juan Hill.

U.S. soldiers had a difficult climb up San Juan Hill. They could not advance safely as Spanish soldiers fired down on them. But the U.S. Army had brought four Gatling guns to the battle site. These hand-cranked machine guns rapidly fired many bullets. U.S. soldiers used these guns to protect troops climbing up San Juan Hill. The Spanish soldiers were forced to retreat to Santiago.

Destruction of the Spanish Fleet

By July 2, Shafter's forces controlled the territory around Santiago. But he felt he needed more artillery to capture the city. He did not want to risk losing many soldiers in an attack on the city.

Shafter sent Admiral Sampson a message. Sampson's fleet blocked the harbor to Santiago. Shafter asked Sampson to fire his ships' cannons at Santiago. But Sampson refused. He did not want to risk losing his ships to mines in the harbor. These floating devices explode when ships sail into them.

On July 3, Sampson and Shafter met at Siboney. They planned an attack on Santiago.

On the same day, Admiral Cervera led the Spanish fleet out of Santiago Bay. Cervera feared that his ships would be captured if they remained in the city's harbor. He also hoped his decision to leave would surprise the U.S. fleet into allowing his ships to escape.

Commodore Schley took command of the U.S. fleet in Sampson's absence. He ordered

The U.S. fleet sank all of the Spanish ships that tried to escape from Santiago Bay.

U.S. ships to chase the Spanish ships. Cannon fire from the U.S. ships' large artillery guns caused much damage to the Spanish ships. The fastest Spanish ship only made it 75 miles (121 kilometers) before being destroyed.

Spanish Surrender in Cuba

On July 10, Shafter met with General José Toral. Toral commanded the Spanish troops in Santiago. He wanted to surrender.

U.S. General Miles arrived in Cuba to join in the peace talks. The U.S. government promised to transport Toral's soldiers to Spain in exchange for his surrender. Toral's officers also would be allowed to keep their horses and swords. Toral accepted these conditions and officially surrendered on July 17.

Puerto Rico

Miles left for Puerto Rico on July 25. Miles sought to gain control of the Spanish-held island. A total of 15,000 U.S. soldiers landed near the town of Guánica.

U.S. troops captured the town of Coamo on August 9. They then marched toward San Juan. This is the capital city of Puerto Rico.

On August 12, news reached Miles that a peace settlement between Spain and the United States had been reached. This ended the fighting in Puerto Rico.

The Trip Home

After Toral's surrender, U.S. officers in Cuba requested that troops be sent home. Many soldiers were becoming sick with malaria, typhoid, and yellow fever. But the U.S. War Department wanted to keep troops in Cuba until a peace treaty was signed with Spain. On July 31, these U.S. officers met and wrote letters to the War Department to repeat their request. Newspapers in the United States received copies of these letters and printed them.

The U.S. government then allowed all soldiers in good health to return. On August 7, transport ships began to carry soldiers of the 5th Army Corps to Montauk Point, New York. Other soldiers were sent home as they recovered from their illnesses.

The Philippines and Guam

During the 1890s, the people of the Philippines formed a group called the Katipunan. This group of rebels worked for the independence of their country. Their leader was General Emilio Aguinaldo.

Commodore Dewey's defeat of the Spanish fleet did not bring him control of the islands. He then blockaded Manila and requested troops from the United States to help in his fight. Dewey also asked Aguinaldo to form a rebel army and fight the Spanish soldiers until U.S. troops arrived. Aguinaldo promised the Katipunan's support to Dewey.

Aguinaldo led the Filipino rebels.

Many Filipino people supported Aguinaldo.
He formed a local government and wrote a
Philippine Declaration of Independence.

In June 1898, Spanish forces were trapped in
Manila. The rebel army surrounded them on land
and Dewey's ships blockaded them at sea.

U.S. troops were sent to the Philippines.

U.S. troops sailed to the Philippines to assist in the fight. On the way, they captured the Spanish-held island of Guam. The Spanish commander there did not even know his government was at war with the United States.

In early July, the first U.S. troops arrived in Manila. General Firmín Jaudenes led the Spanish troops in Manila. He surrendered on August 13, 1898.

The United States took control of the Philippines. But many Filipinos opposed U.S.

forces staying on their islands. Aguinaldo and his rebels then revolted against the United States. This war is known as the Philippine Insurrection (1899–1902). Filipinos call it the War for Independence. More than 4,000 U.S. troops and 16,000 Filipinos died in the fighting.

On July 4, 1902, the U.S. Army defeated the rebels. Aguinaldo promised to allow the United States to build naval bases in the Philippines. He also gave control of trade to the United States.

Peace Treaty of Paris

On September 26, 1898, Spanish and U.S. diplomats met in Paris, France. They met to discuss the terms for a peace treaty. The Treaty of Paris was signed on December 10, 1898.

The U.S. now controlled overseas colonies as many European countries did. The islands of Guam and Puerto Rico became U.S. territories. The peace treaty also allowed the United States to buy the Philippines from Spain.

Cuba gained its independence from Spain. But some U.S. forces remained in Cuba. The United States built a naval base at Guantánamo. Many Cubans were opposed to this. They did not want U.S. troops to remain in their country.

Timeline

October—Ten Years' War (1868–78) begins.

February—Spanish soldiers begin to force villagers into "reconcentrado" camps.

January —Cubans riot in Havana. McKinley sends the battleship *Maine* there to protect U.S. citizens in Havana.

1868

1896

1898

1895

1897

February—The *Maine* explodes in Havana's harbor.

March—William McKinley begins his first term as President of the United States.

February—Second war for Cuban independence begins.

Spanish-American War

April—McKinley asks Congress for a declaration of war against Spain. He then orders a naval blockade around Cuba. McKinley also asks 125,000 volunteers to enlist in the army.

June—U.S. troops land at Guantánamo. They also land at Daiquirí and Siboney. Battle of Las Guásimas takes place. U.S. troops capture the island of Guam.

December—Treaty of Paris is signed in Paris, France.

1898

May—George Dewey attacks Spanish ships in the Philippines. The 8th Army Corps is sent to the Philippines. Spanish ships from Spain arrive in Santiago Harbor. U.S. ships blockade the harbor.

July—U.S. troops attack El Caney. They also attack San Juan Hill and Kettle Hill. The Spanish fleet is destroyed trying to escape Santiago Harbor. Spanish forces at Santiago surrender. U.S. troops occupy the island of Puerto Rico.

Words to Know

artillery (ar-TIL-uh-ree)—a unit of soldiers who use cannons in battle

blockade (blok-ADE)—closing off an area to keep people or supplies from passing through

cavalry (CAV-uhl-ree)—a unit of soldiers who fight on horseback

division (di-VIZH-uhn)—a military unit made up of several smaller units called regiments

enlist (en-LIST)—to join the military

infantry (IN-fuhn-tree)—a unit of soldiers who fight on foot

ration (RASH-uhn)—daily amount of food given to a soldier

regiment (REJ-uh-muhnt)—a military unit consisting of about 1,000 soldiers

To Learn More

Carter, Alden R. *The Spanish-American War: Imperial Ambitions.* A First Book. New York: Franklin Watts, 1992.

Collins, Mary. *The Spanish-American War.* Cornerstones of Freedom. New York: Children's Press, 1998.

Gay, Kathlyn. *Spanish-American War.* Voices From the Past. New York: Twenty-First Century Books, 1995.

Schuman, Michael. *Theodore Roosevelt.* United States Presidents. Springfield, N.J.: Enslow Publishers, 1997.

Useful Addresses

Independence Seaport Museum
Penn's Landing
211 South Columbus Boulevard
Philadelphia, PA 19106-3199

National McKinley Birthplace Memorial
40 North Main Street
Niles, OH 44446

Sagamore Hill National Historic Site
20 Sagamore Hill Road
Oyster Bay, NY 11771-1807

Internet Sites

Visit the FactHound at *www.facthound.com*

All the FactHound sites are hand-selected by our editors. FactHound will fetch the best, most accurate information to answer your questions.

IT'S EASY! IT'S FUN!
1) Go to *www.facthound.com*
2) Type in: **0736805834**
3) Click on **FETCH IT** and FactHound will put you on the trail of several helpful links.

You can also search by subject or book title. So, relax and let our pal FactHound do the research for you!

Index